THE SILENCE THAT KILLS

Master Crisis Communications in a Noisy World

Nikki Wheeler

THE STORM THAT CHANGED EVERYTHING

It was just before dawn when the first whispers of trouble began to trickle through the office. Sarah, the communications director at a mid-sized pharmaceutical company, was sipping her morning coffee when her phone buzzed. She glanced at the screen and saw the alert: *"Potential safety breach in production facility."* It was vague but enough to jolt her into action. Little did she know, the next few hours would test every skill, decision, and piece of knowledge she had about managing a crisis.

The company, HealthPoint Labs, was known for producing affordable over-the-counter medications. Their latest product, a fever-reducing syrup for children, had seen record sales since its release. But now, rumors were starting to circulate online that batches of the syrup might be contaminated with harmful chemicals. It was only 6:30 a.m., and already, customers were posting concerned messages on social media. Local news stations were starting to ask questions. As parents across the region began to worry, HealthPoint's crisis team scrambled to make sense of the unfolding situation.

Sarah knew her response needed to be fast, clear, and above all, truthful. But there was a problem: the executives weren't ready to confirm any contamination. They insisted on waiting until the production team could run full diagnostics—a process that could take hours, if not days. She tried to explain the company's silence might be read as indifference or incompetence, but her arguments were brushed aside. The head of operations suggested a holding statement, something vague about "quality control procedures," but Sarah knew it wouldn't reassure the public or quell the rising panic.

By noon, the story had spread like wildfire. Parents were demanding refunds and filing complaints, retailers were pulling the product from shelves, and HealthPoint's stock price had taken a nosedive. News crews were camping outside the production facility, seeking any scrap of information. Desperate, Sarah proposed holding a press conference to explain what they did know and what measures they were taking. But again, she was overruled. "It will only fuel the fire," the CEO insisted.

That afternoon, the worst happened. An independent lab had run its own tests and announced it had found traces of the contaminant in the syrup. The media pounced on the report, and within minutes, HealthPoint was a national story for all the wrong reasons. Sarah felt the weight of every missed opportunity, every warning she'd issued to her superiors, every decision to withhold information. What had begun as a manageable crisis had escalated into a full-blown disaster.

Looking back, Sarah would later reflect on how different things could have been if HealthPoint had faced the problem head-on. A timely acknowledgment, an expression of genuine concern, and transparent communication might have turned a panicked public into an understanding one. Instead, by hiding behind caution and hesitation, they had lost control over the story and, worse, the trust of their customers.

The HealthPoint crisis serves as a case study in how not to manage risk and crisis communication—a sobering reminder that in a world where information spreads at the speed of a tweet, the cost of silence is far greater than the cost of transparency. Because in times of crisis, it isn't just what you say, but how and when you say it, that shapes your organization's fate.

www.ingramcontent.com/pod-product-compliance
Lightning Source LLC
Chambersburg PA
CBHW071517220526
45472CB00003B/1059

About This Playbook

As *The Storm that Changed Everything*, illustrates, in an increasingly interconnected and fast-paced world, a crisis can hit any organization at any time—often without warning. Crisis management is the structured process of addressing and responding to major events or situations that threaten to harm an organization, its stakeholders, and the public.

The rapid, effective management of these incidents is critical to safeguarding an organization's reputation, minimizing financial losses, and protecting the trust it holds with its audiences. But within crisis management, one area often makes the difference between resilience and irreparable damage: communication.

A crisis communications playbook is a vital reference tool designed to guide organizations through the unpredictable, high-stakes world of crisis communication. Unlike a strict blueprint, it doesn't prescribe one-size-fits-all solutions. Rather, it serves as a flexible, strategic resource—one that can be adapted to various situations and scaled depending on the crisis level and organizational needs.

This playbook is about preparation and adaptability, empowering teams to respond swiftly and effectively to whatever comes their way. Here's what this Crisis Communications Playbook covers:

1. **Descriptions of Different Levels of Crisis:** Not all crises are created equal. Some can be contained with quick, direct action, while others escalate rapidly, spreading through social media or news outlets, demanding broader, more complex responses. This playbook breaks down

the levels of crisis, from minor disruptions to full-scale reputational emergencies, helping teams assess the scope and severity of an incident. Understanding these levels is crucial for tailoring responses that are proportionate to the situation, avoiding overreaction or, worse, a delayed or underwhelming response.

2. **An Overview of How to Manage Various Crises**: Effective crisis management isn't just about responding in the moment; it's also about knowing the best practices that have proven effective across industries and types of crises. This playbook provides high-level guidance on managing crises across several scenarios, such as product recalls, data breaches, workplace accidents, and public relations missteps. For each scenario, it offers foundational principles to guide decision-making, from assessing the initial threat to deploying the right message to the right audiences at the right time.

3. **Roles and Responsibilities**: During a crisis, everyone from executives to frontline staff has a role to play, but clarity is essential to avoid confusion and ensure a streamlined response. This playbook outlines the roles and responsibilities across key players in the organization, helping teams understand who does what when the stakes are high. By pre-assigning roles and establishing a clear chain of command, this playbook helps eliminate the "fog of crisis," where roles blur under pressure, ensuring everyone is aligned and focused on their specific duties.

4. **Recommendations for Actions During a Crisis:** The playbook doesn't just describe what a crisis looks like; it also offers actionable recommendations for each stage of the crisis lifecycle, from preparation and response to recovery. In the first moments of a crisis, when every decision counts, having pre-established, research-backed recommendations can make all the difference. This

playbook advises on immediate response actions, tone of messaging, handling media inquiries, and leveraging digital platforms. It also provides insights on when and how to escalate the crisis response, communicate directly with stakeholders, and evaluate the effectiveness of the response.

Why This Playbook Matters

The need for a well-developed Crisis Communications Playbook has never been greater. In today's "always-on" media landscape, a single incident can turn into a public relations nightmare within hours, if not minutes.

Organizations that are prepared with clear guidelines, tested protocols, and flexible communication strategies stand a far better chance of not only surviving a crisis but emerging with their reputation intact or even strengthened. This playbook is your organization's toolkit for navigating these turbulent waters —a resource to prevent minor crises from spiraling out of control, preserve public trust, and ultimately protect the organization's mission and future.

By leveraging this playbook, your team gains the structure and confidence needed to approach any crisis with clarity, cohesion, and purpose.

Disclaimer:

Before we dive into the world of crisis communications, here's something important you should know: all the companies, characters, and scenarios in this book are fictionalized composites. Think of them as "greatest hits" from crisis communications mishaps and victories I've witnessed over the past twenty-five-plus years, mixed with a dash of drama, suspense, and just enough realism to make you question your own plan.

While the tales and scenarios may feel uncannily familiar, they're designed to highlight the principles of crisis and risk communication without exposing real individuals or companies who may still be navigating these stormy waters. So, if any story sounds a little too close to home—don't worry. It's purely coincidental. Your secrets are still safe with me.

It's also essential to note, nothing in this playbook constitutes legal advice. The playbook and recommendations are informational and educational tools to help you think critically about crisis communications. Every organization's needs and risks are unique, and it's up to you to adapt these concepts responsibly, considering the specific legal and regulatory requirements of your industry.

With that out of the way, grab a coffee (and maybe a notepad) and get ready to learn from these "hypothetical" disasters. Because, as they say, it's much more fun to learn from someone else's crisis than to live through one yourself.

PART I: CRISIS COMMUNICATIONS ESSENTIALS

The Cost of Silence

I t was a typical Monday morning at *Aspire Electronics*, a well-respected manufacturer of consumer gadgets. The CEO, Linda, had just finished her coffee when her phone rang. On the other end was her head of product development, with a look of panic in his voice: *"We have a major issue. Some of our devices are overheating and catching fire."*

Linda's stomach dropped. Aspire Electronics had built its reputation on reliability and safety. A defect like this was more than a technical glitch—it was a potential disaster for their brand. But before she could process the full scope of the problem, Linda's PR advisor, Eric, suggested they wait and gather more data before making any public statements. "Let's not jump the gun," Eric said. "We don't want to cause unnecessary alarm."

Linda, unsure of the best course of action, agreed. For the next two days, they chose silence, hoping that the issue was minor and isolated. But in the age of social media, word traveled quickly. Videos of smoking devices started surfacing online, and the news was soon picked up by major media outlets. Customers, furious at Aspire's lack of transparency, took to social media, criticizing the company for ignoring safety concerns. The hashtag #AspireBurnout began trending.

By the time Linda and her team issued their first statement, it was too late. The narrative had spiraled out of their control. Their vague response only fueled public outrage, as customers and media outlets demanded accountability and transparency. Aspire's competitors seized the opportunity, emphasizing their commitment to safety in their own marketing messages. Within a week, Aspire Electronics' stock had plummeted, and retailers began pulling their products from shelves.

According to Deloitte, a mishandled crisis can lead to a 30% decrease in market value within just a few weeks. Aspire Electronics experienced this firsthand as their market value tumbled, costing the company millions. The financial damage didn't stop there. The International Risk Management Institute (IRMI) estimates that companies can lose up to $4.3 million on average in reputation and brand damage following a poorly managed crisis. Aspire's reputation was now in tatters and repairing it would take years.

But the worst news came from their financial advisors, who warned that Aspire might not recover from this blow for a long time. Research from the Oxford Executive Research Group shows that companies mismanaging a crisis can take up to five years to recover their stock price. For Linda and her team, the price of silence and hesitation was staggering, and they were left to wonder how things might have turned out differently had they acted sooner and more decisively.

Aspire Electronics' story is a powerful reminder that effective crisis communication isn't just about protecting reputation; it's essential for financial survival. In this chapter, we'll cover the essentials of crisis communication—principles that could have saved Aspire Electronics from the worst of their ordeal.

In the realm of crisis management, response timing, and clarity can be the difference between swift resolution and prolonged damage. This chapter, Crisis Communications Essentials, provides the foundational information needed to assess, classify, and act upon a crisis situation as it unfolds. The information outlined here serves as a reference guide for quick assessment, enabling your team to determine whether immediate action is required and if full activation of the Crisis Communications Playbook is necessary.

When facing a potential crisis, having a clear, structured approach ensures that your response is proportionate to the severity of the issue. This chapter introduces the three crisis classification levels, as well as guidelines on immediate actions based on urgency, providing the essential framework for making rapid, informed decisions.

I. ESSENTIAL INFORMATION FOR CRISIS CLASSIFICATION

Crises don't all share the same impact or urgency, and distinguishing between them allows your team to allocate resources and attention appropriately. This chapter defines three levels of crisis—Minor, Moderate, and Major Risk—based on potential impacts on the organization, stakeholders, and public perception. Each level comes with specific actions and communication protocols tailored to the gravity of the situation.

Crisis Classification Levels

1. **Level 1 - Minor**
   - **Definition**: A Level 1 crisis is a minor issue with limited impact, usually confined to:
     - A single facility
     - A very limited number of customers, suppliers, or members of the community
   - **Characteristics**:
     - Does not include regulatory, customer, or authority concerns.
     - Typically, does not attract media attention.
     - Can be managed through regular departmental

processes without external escalation.

- ■ **Examples**: Minor operational delays, isolated equipment malfunctions, or limited customer complaints that do not affect overall business operations.

2. **Level 2 - Moderate Risk**
   - **Definition**: A Level 2 crisis presents a moderate risk and may have a more noticeable impact on:
     - Day-to-day business activities or operations affecting multiple stakeholders.
     - Limited production issues that do not threaten long-term viability but require intervention.
   - **Characteristics**:
     - Potentially temporary disruption with the ability to resume normal business activities in less than 30 days.
     - May draw some media attention.
     - Requires notification to the Crisis Communications team as a "FYI," but may not require immediate action.
       - ■ **Examples**: Temporary shutdown of a production line affecting customer delivery schedules, limited negative press coverage, or minor regulatory inquiries.

3. **Level 3 - Major Risk**
   - **Definition**: A Level 3 crisis is a significant threat with severe impact, affecting:
     - The organization's day-to-day activities and operations.
     - Multiple facilities, and possibly the ability to ship and produce products.
     - The organization's reputation or financial stability.
   - **Characteristics**:
     - Major business interruptions, product recalls, potential fatalities, or large-scale destruction.

- ◦ Likely to attract ongoing media coverage, possibly at a national or international level.
- ◦ Requires immediate activation of the Crisis Communications team and senior leadership.
  - ▪ **Examples**: Widespread product recalls, serious workplace accidents involving

II. Crisis Communications Action Guide

The Crisis Communications Action Guide provides structured, level-specific actions based on the urgency of the situation. Use this guide to determine the appropriate escalation level and immediate steps required. In cases where a situation falls between two levels, it is best practice to classify it at the higher level and follow those corresponding guidelines.

Crisis Classification and Urgency-Based Actions

The chart below outlines crisis response actions by classification level and urgency, specifying when to notify the Crisis Communications team and when to escalate the issue through internal chains of command.

Crisis Classification Level	High	Medium	Low
Level 3 - Major Risk	**Immediate action**: Contact executive member and initiate a Crisis Communications team meeting.	Escalate issue through functional/ customer segment chain within **4 hours**. Notify Crisis Communications team within **4 hours**.	Escalate issue through functional/customer segment chain within **4 hours**. Notify Crisis Communications team within **4 hours**.
Level 2	Escalate issue	Escalate issue	Escalate issue through

- Moderate Risk	through functional/customer segment chain **immediately**. Notify Crisis Communications team immediately.	through functional/customer segment chain within **4 hours**. Notify Crisis Communications team as "FYI."	functional/customer segment chain within **48 hours**. Notify Crisis Communications team as "FYI."
Level 1 - Minor Risk	Manage issue through functional/customer segment chain of command.	Manage issue through functional/customer segment chain of command.	Manage issue through functional/customer segment chain of command.

Understanding Urgency Levels

The urgency level of a crisis affects how quickly action should be taken, particularly when notifying the Crisis Communications team and escalating through the organizational hierarchy.

- **High**: Impact is already underway or highly likely to occur within **24 hours**. Immediate, urgent action at the highest level is required.
- **Medium**: Impact is likely to occur within **1 to 5 days**. Action should be taken within 4 hours, with an FYI to the Crisis Communications team.
- **Low**: Impact is not likely to occur within **5 days**. Issue can be managed within the normal chain of command but may still require same-day action.

Best Practice: If there is any potential for media coverage at any level, it is best to engage the Crisis Communications team as a proactive measure.

III. Crisis Communications Best Practices

Beyond immediate actions and classifications, certain best practices should be upheld across all crisis levels to ensure consistent, transparent, and effective communication:

- **Act with Transparency**: Being open and clear with stakeholders is crucial, even when all the information is not yet available. Transparency builds trust and can mitigate backlash.

- **Monitor Media and Public Sentiment**: Social and traditional media play significant roles in shaping public perception. Monitor these channels closely to stay ahead of potential issues and adjust messaging as needed.

- **Respond with Empathy**: Remember that a crisis often impacts people directly. Acknowledge their concerns and emotions in your communication to humanize your response and maintain goodwill.

- **Document and Review**: Each crisis offers valuable lessons. Document decisions, actions, and outcomes for future reference and review. After the crisis, conduct a full evaluation to improve response strategies.

IV. When to Activate the Full Crisis Communications Playbook

While not all incidents require activating the full Crisis Communications Playbook, certain indicators suggest it is necessary:

- **Significant Reputational or Financial Threats**: If a crisis is likely to affect the organization's reputation, market value, or customer base in a serious way.

- **Persistent Media Coverage**: If media attention persists beyond a single news cycle, suggesting a need for coordinated, ongoing response efforts.

- **Cross-Functional Impact**: If the crisis affects multiple departments or functions, requiring a unified approach to communication and strategy.
- **Stakeholder Demands**: If stakeholders such as customers, partners, or regulators demand an explanation or corrective action, activate the playbook to ensure a cohesive response.

This Crisis Communications Essentials chapter equips you with the knowledge to quickly assess, classify, and act upon potential crises. The guidelines provided here streamline initial crisis assessment, clarify immediate actions based on urgency, and reinforce best practices that can be applied universally. In the chapters that follow, we'll delve deeper into each phase of crisis communication, from preparation and execution to evaluation and recovery, building on this essential foundation.

Key Takeaways:

1. **Understand Crisis Classification**: Not all crises are the same. By classifying crises as Minor, Moderate, or Major Risk, organizations can allocate resources and attention based on the level of impact and urgency. This classification system enables efficient, proportionate responses.

2. **Differentiate Urgency Levels**: Urgency plays a critical role in determining response speed. High urgency requires immediate action, Medium urgency suggests response within a few hours, and Low urgency allows for a more measured approach within the chain of command.

3. **Level-Specific Actions**:
   - **Level 1 - Minor Risk**: Handled within regular departmental processes without involving the Crisis Communications team unless necessary.
   - **Level 2 - Moderate Risk**: May impact day-to-day operations and attract some media attention. Requires communication with the Crisis Communications team as an FYI, with potential escalation based on urgency.
   - **Level 3 - Major Risk**: Poses severe impact on operations, reputation, or safety. Requires immediate activation of the Crisis Communications team and involvement of senior leadership.

4. **Follow Best Practices Consistently**:
   - **Act with Transparency**: Openness with stakeholders builds trust, even when all information isn't yet available.
   - **Monitor Media and Public Sentiment**: Proactively track social and traditional media to manage public perception and respond to emerging narratives.
   - **Respond with Empathy**: Crises affect people directly;

acknowledging their concerns humanizes the response.

- **Document and Review**: Every crisis provides lessons. Documenting actions and outcomes supports continuous improvement and better preparedness for future crises.

5. **Know When to Activate the Full Crisis Communications Playbook**: Activation is warranted when there are significant reputational or financial threats, persistent media coverage, cross-functional impact, or clear demands from stakeholders.

Action Items:

1. **Implement Crisis Classification System**:
   - Develop internal guidelines that define Level 1 (Minor), Level 2 (Moderate), and Level 3 (Major) crises. Ensure that all team members understand how to classify crises and the specific actions required at each level.
   - Conduct training sessions to help staff recognize and respond appropriately based on crisis classification.

2. **Establish Urgency Protocols**:
   - Set clear guidelines for High, Medium, and Low urgency situations and ensure they are accessible to all teams.
   - Develop a rapid escalation process for High urgency crises, enabling swift notification of the Crisis Communications team and senior leadership.

3. **Create a Crisis Communications Action Guide**:
   - Draft a guide with step-by-step actions for each crisis level and urgency level, specifying when to escalate and whom to notify.
   - Review and update the guide periodically based on feedback and evolving best practices.

4. **Reinforce Best Practices in Crisis Communication**:
   - Integrate transparency, media monitoring, empathy, and documentation into every crisis response process.
   - Assign specific team members to handle media monitoring and social listening during crises to stay ahead of public perception and address misinformation promptly.

5. **Define Triggers for Full Playbook Activation**:
   - Outline specific indicators that require activation of the full Crisis Communications Playbook, such as high-impact media coverage, reputational threats, or stakeholder demands.

- Ensure all team members are aware of these triggers and know how to escalate the response if these conditions arise.

6. **Review and Practice Crisis Communication Protocols**:
   - Conduct regular simulations and drills to practice crisis classification, urgency-based actions, and playbook activation.
   - After each drill or real crisis, conduct a review session to assess performance, identify improvement areas, and document lessons learned.

By following these key takeaways and action items, organizations can create a robust crisis response framework, ensuring that they respond to crises with precision, empathy, and transparency while preserving public trust and operational integrity.

BUILDING THE CRISIS COMMUNICATIONS MANAGEMENT TEAM

The Unprepared CEO

I t was a bright Tuesday morning at *GreenTech Innovations*, a rapidly growing company in the renewable energy sector. The CEO, Richard, was in the middle of a strategy meeting with his leadership team when his phone buzzed with an urgent text: *"We have a problem."* The message was from the head of operations, and before Richard could reply, another message came through. This one had a photo attached: a fiery plume of smoke rising from one of GreenTech's largest solar farms.

Panic spread through the room as word of the incident circulated. Richard was used to tackling challenges head-on, but this was different. There were already news trucks gathering outside the office, and social media was buzzing with speculation about safety and environmental impact. Richard glanced around the table, looking to his team for guidance, but they seemed just as lost as he was. No one knew who should handle the media inquiries, how to address employee concerns, or what safety measures to communicate to the public.

As the minutes ticked by, it became clear that GreenTech Innovations had no crisis management structure in place. They were one of the many organizations that, despite their best intentions, had never formalized a crisis communications team or process. Richard felt the weight of the situation as he realized how unprepared they truly were. Despite all the talk about growth, sustainability, and innovation, no one had taken the time to plan for a crisis of this magnitude.

Later, after the dust had settled, Richard would learn that GreenTech's experience wasn't unique. According to PWC's Global Crisis Survey 2021, 69% of organizations have experienced at least one crisis in the past five years, with most facing an average of three crises. Yet, despite these rising occurrences, only 23% of organizations feel they are "very prepared" for a major crisis (BCG Global Crisis Management Survey, 2021). Unfortunately, GreenTech was among the 77% of companies that hadn't taken proactive steps to prepare for the unexpected.

Richard's ordeal was a wake-up call. He realized that if his company was to survive future crises, he needed to build a dedicated Crisis Communications Management Team—a team of trusted leaders with clearly defined roles and responsibilities to guide GreenTech through even the most turbulent times. This chapter will explore how organizations can avoid the same pitfalls that Richard faced by assembling and training a crisis communications team that is ready to act decisively and effectively, no matter what crisis may arise.

In times of crisis, the strength and coordination of the Crisis Communications Management Team (CCMT) are critical to ensuring a swift, organized, and effective response. This chapter explores the structure, roles, and responsibilities of the Crisis Communications Team and the Core Crisis Management Team, detailing how these teams work in tandem to address both operational and communicative aspects of a crisis.

I. CRISIS COMMUNICATIONS TEAM COMPOSITION

The Crisis Communications Team is a cross-functional group composed of key executive leaders who bring expertise from essential areas within the organization. Their combined skills, insights, and authority allow the team to quickly assess, decide, and execute the organization's crisis communication strategy.

Core Team Members

The core team includes leaders from:

- **Communications**: Oversees all messaging, ensures consistent communication, and liaises with media outlets.
- **Marketing**: Monitors brand implications and ensures that the organization's reputation is protected and preserved.
- **Legal**: Provides guidance on compliance, legal risks, and regulatory issues, ensuring that all public statements align with legal requirements.
- **Operations**: Ensures continuity of business functions and coordinates the logistics of the organization's operational response.
- **Public Policy**: Handles any interactions with government or regulatory bodies and ensures that all communications align with current public policy considerations.

- **Human Resources**: Manages communication with employees, addresses workforce concerns, and provides support related to internal issues that may arise.

Extended Team Members

For significant crises that require elevated support, the core team may call upon:

- **The President and Chief Executive Officer (CEO)**: Represents the organization at the highest level and may serve as the spokesperson if the situation demands top-level visibility.
- **The Chief Financial Officer (CFO)**: Offers insight into the financial implications of the crisis and ensures that the organization's fiscal health and responsibilities are considered in all decisions.

Regional and Local Facility Support

Depending on the nature and scale of the crisis, the core team may also enlist regional leads and local facilities teams. These individuals provide insights from specific locations, facilitating communication that is relevant, timely, and responsive to regional concerns. Regional and local team members are invaluable in tailoring the organization's message to the specific needs of impacted areas, as well as ensuring that communication aligns with local sensitivities.

II. Roles and Responsibilities

The Crisis Communications Management Team is organized into two distinct yet complementary teams: the Core Crisis Management Team and the Crisis Communications Team. Together, they manage the overall crisis response, from operations to communication, ensuring both the logistics of the crisis response and the delivery of a consistent, reassuring message.

Core Crisis Management Team

The Core Crisis Management Team is responsible for managing the activity surrounding the crisis itself, focusing on operational issues, fact-finding, and coordinating resources.

Key Responsibilities:

- **Identification and Assessment**: Recognize the crisis, confirm its details, and gauge its impact on the organization, stakeholders, and public.
- **Decision-Making and Recommendations**: Make decisions and propose actions based on gathered information and expert consultations.
- **Resource Coordination**: Ensure necessary resources are available, including personnel, equipment, and information.
- **Stakeholder Communication**: Identify key internal and external individuals who need to be informed or consulted, such as employees, partners, and critical vendors.
- **Consultation with Experts**: Engage with internal and external experts for specialized advice on handling the crisis, from security experts to industry consultants.
- **Operational Execution**: Authorize and implement actions that contain and mitigate the impact of the crisis,

stabilizing operations as needed.

- **Customer Notification**: Communicate with customers to keep them informed about the organization's response and any potential impact on services or products.

Crisis Communications Team

The Crisis Communications Team is tasked with managing communication activities surrounding the crisis, ensuring that both internal and external messaging aligns with the organization's values and objectives. This team focuses on preserving the organization's reputation, informing stakeholders, and maintaining public trust.

Key Responsibilities:

- **Information Gathering**: Collect facts to accurately address the crisis with key stakeholders, including customers, partners, and the media.
- **Stakeholder Identification and Communication**: Determine the individuals and groups affected by the crisis and craft messages tailored to their needs and concerns.
- **Media Relations**: Engage with media outlets, provide regular updates, and monitor media coverage to stay ahead of the narrative and manage misinformation.
- **Decision-Making on Communication Strategy**: Make recommendations and decisions regarding how, when, and what information should be shared, ensuring that all messaging is consistent, factual, and empathetic.
- **Internal Notifications**: Collaborate with the Internal Communications team to prepare messages for employees, ensuring staff remain informed, unified, and engaged.
- **Leadership Support**: Keep executive leadership informed on communication strategy, media responses, and public sentiment to enable informed decision-making at the

highest levels.

III. Functional Responsibilities in Crisis Communication

To effectively manage both operational and communicative aspects of a crisis, the responsibilities of each team member are divided based on their area of expertise, creating a cohesive response strategy that addresses both immediate needs and long-term consequences.

Identification and Assessment of the Crisis

- The Core Crisis Management Team identifies an actual situation or problem, assessing its scope, urgency, and potential impact. By evaluating the level of risk (Minor, Moderate, Major), this team sets the stage for a proportional response.
- The Crisis Communications Team gathers relevant facts about the crisis from a communications perspective, ensuring that any public messaging is based on accurate, verified information.

Recommendations for Action

- The Core Team makes recommendations based on operational needs, legal considerations, and the necessity to minimize disruption to normal business activities.
- The Communications Team advises on the best approach to communicate these decisions to stakeholders, factoring in potential legal, financial, and market implications.

Legal, Financial, and Market Considerations

Both teams consult the Legal and Financial departments to weigh the broader implications of decisions, such as potential liabilities or financial impacts. This ensures that the organization is protected from future legal or financial fallout while preserving public trust.

Developing the Crisis Communications Plan

- Depending on the severity of the crisis, the Crisis Communications Team develops a crisis communications plan, which includes:

  - **Defining Key Messages**: Establishing clear and consistent corporate messaging that aligns with the organization's values and addresses stakeholder concerns.

  - **Designating Spokespersons**: Selecting appropriate representatives to communicate on behalf of the organization, ensuring that messaging is delivered with authority and empathy.

  - **Determining Communication Channels**: Identifying the most effective channels (e.g., press releases, social media, email notifications) to reach different stakeholders promptly.

  - **Setting a Communication Timeline**: Establishing a timeline for regular updates to keep stakeholders informed as the crisis unfolds and as new information becomes available.

Participation and Consultation

- Participation by each team member is determined by the crisis situation and level. In some cases, a rapid response may require only the core team, while in larger or more complex crises, additional stakeholders from regional offices or external consultants may need to be brought in.

- Team members consult with each other as well as with external advisors and experts, ensuring that all perspectives are considered when developing the crisis management and communication strategies.

IV. Working Together: Coordinating the Crisis Response

For a crisis response to be effective, the Core Crisis Management Team and Crisis Communications Team must operate in sync, sharing information, coordinating actions, and ensuring all stakeholders receive consistent, accurate messaging. Here's how these teams collaborate:

1. **Unified Fact-Gathering**: Both teams work together to compile all known facts about the crisis. This ensures that both operational decisions and public messaging are based on the same information.

2. **Coordinated Decision-Making**: While the Core Team may make decisions about operational responses, the Communications Team is responsible for interpreting these decisions into actionable communication strategies that preserve the organization's credibility.

3. **Consistent Messaging**: The Communications Team collaborates with the Core Team to ensure that internal and external stakeholders receive consistent information, reducing the potential for misunderstandings or conflicting statements.

4. **Monitoring and Feedback Loop**: The Communications Team monitors media coverage and public sentiment, providing feedback to the Core Team about the effectiveness of the response. This real-time feedback loop allows the team to adjust strategies as needed and stay ahead of evolving narratives.

5. **Leadership Involvement**: For significant crises, top leadership—such as the CEO and CFO—are briefed regularly to provide oversight, represent the organization if needed, and approve key decisions.

V. THE IMPORTANCE OF TEAM READINESS

The effectiveness of a Crisis Communications Management Team depends on its readiness and coordination. Regular training, simulations, and post-crisis debriefings are essential to ensure that all team members understand their roles, know how to work together, and can execute a rapid, unified response under pressure. An organization's reputation, stakeholder trust, and even its survival can hinge on the preparedness of its crisis management teams.

In summary, building a capable, cross-functional Crisis Communications Management Team is foundational to an organization's resilience. By assembling experts from key areas, defining clear roles, and fostering collaboration between the Core Crisis Management Team and Crisis Communications Team, organizations can be better prepared to address crises swiftly and communicate effectively. This ensures not only operational continuity but also the maintenance of public trust and reputation, ultimately safeguarding the organization's future.

Key Takeaways:

1. **Crisis Communications Team Composition**: A cross-functional Crisis Communications Team is essential for effective crisis response. Core team members should come from Communications, Marketing, Legal, Operations, Public Policy, and Human Resources, with extended support from senior leadership (CEO, CFO) as needed.

2. **Roles and Responsibilities**: The team is split into the Core Crisis Management Team (handling operational response and logistics) and the Crisis Communications Team (managing internal and external messaging). Each has specific, complementary roles, ensuring a comprehensive approach to crisis management.

3. **Functional Responsibilities**: Each team member's role is defined based on their expertise, allowing the Core Crisis Management Team to focus on operational continuity and the Crisis Communications Team to focus on effective, empathetic communication.

4. **Coordination and Collaboration**: For a cohesive response, both teams must work in sync. They share facts, coordinate decisions, and ensure consistent messaging, with feedback loops for real-time adjustments.

5. **Leadership Involvement**: In major crises, senior leaders like the CEO and CFO are essential for high-level decisions and as spokespersons, adding credibility and authority to the organization's response.

6. **Team Readiness**: Preparedness is key. Regular training, simulations, and post-crisis debriefings strengthen team readiness, ensuring swift, coordinated responses that protect the organization's reputation and stakeholder

trust.

Action Items:

1. **Assemble the Crisis Communications Team**: Identify and formally assign members to the core Crisis Communications Team and extended team. Ensure representation from Communications, Marketing, Legal, Operations, Public Policy, and Human Resources.

2. **Define Roles Clearly**: Outline each team member's role and responsibilities in the crisis communications plan. Ensure everyone understands their specific duties and the importance of their contributions to the team's overall objectives.

3. **Develop a Crisis Communications Playbook**: Create a playbook that includes protocols, communication channels, messaging templates, and guidelines for each crisis level (Minor, Moderate, Major).

4. **Schedule Regular Training and Simulations**: Conduct crisis response drills and simulations regularly. Include both the Core Crisis Management Team and Crisis Communications Team to practice coordinated responses and refine processes.

5. **Set Up a Communication Feedback Loop**: Establish a protocol for monitoring media and public sentiment, allowing the Crisis Communications Team to relay insights back to the Core Crisis Management Team. Use this feedback to adjust strategies as needed.

6. **Prepare Spokesperson Protocols**: Designate spokespersons for different types of crises and ensure they receive media training. Outline when the CEO or CFO should step in as the face of the organization.

7. **Review and Update the Plan Regularly**: Periodically

review the crisis communications plan, roles, and responsibilities. Adjust based on organizational changes, feedback from past incidents, or emerging best practices in crisis management.

8. **Foster Cross-Functional Collaboration**: Encourage team members to understand each other's roles. This mutual understanding enhances communication and ensures a seamless response during an actual crisis.

By following these takeaways and action items, organizations can build a resilient Crisis Communications Team that is prepared to manage crises with precision, empathy, and authority, safeguarding both the organization's operations and its reputation.

PART II: PRE-CRISIS - THE IMPORTANCE OF PREPARATION

The Summit Software Slam

I magine this: It's a normal Friday afternoon at *Summit Software Solutions*, a bustling tech company specializing in project management tools.

The team is wrapping up for the weekend, and the CEO, Dave, is already talking about hitting the golf course first thing Saturday morning. The vibe is relaxed. But then, with about ten minutes left in the workday, someone in the IT department notices a strange pop-up on their screen. Within minutes, screens across the office start flashing the same message: *"Your files have been encrypted. Pay $100,000 in Bitcoin to regain access."* Summit Software has just been hit with ransomware.

Dave, in a moment of panic, huddles the entire team into the conference room. Everyone looks to him, hoping for guidance, but the truth is, Summit Software has no crisis plan. No one knows who to call, what to say to the media, or how to even address their customers about the impending data breach. Dave, usually the confident leader, stands there, wide-eyed, mumbling about "trying to get someone on the phone."

Eventually, they manage to contact a cybersecurity firm, but the hours of delay have already taken their toll. By the time they start addressing the breach, customers have already noticed something is wrong, and it doesn't take long for the story to spread online.

If only Summit Software had taken a few simple steps to prepare for the unexpected, they might have avoided a lot of embarrassment—and a lot of angry customers. A 2021 Deloitte study found that 38% of companies still lack a crisis communication plan, despite the surge in crisis events. That means nearly four in ten companies are in a position just like Summit Software was: unprepared, disorganized, and exposed.

The story of Summit Software illustrates an important point: preparation is critical. Today every organization must have a solid crisis communications plan and a well-trained team to handle unexpected challenges. According to the Reputation Institute, 63% of companies now view reputational risk management—including crisis communications—as one of their top strategic priorities.

Let's dive into the essential steps that can help you prepare for any crisis, so your organization doesn't end up like Dave's.

THE BUILDING BLOCKS OF EFFECTIVE PREPARATION

Preparation is the cornerstone of successful crisis management. The best way to handle a crisis is to be prepared for one before it even begins.

Pre-crisis preparation involves laying the groundwork for a crisis response, training the team, and conducting realistic exercises to test the Crisis Communications Playbook.

Here are the essential steps that every organization should take to ensure they are ready for the unexpected.

1. Create and Maintain the Crisis Communications Plan

The Crisis Communications Plan is the backbone of your crisis response. It is a dynamic document that outlines the specific steps to take in the event of different types of crises. The plan should be tailored to your organization's unique vulnerabilities, which can range from data breaches and product recalls to natural disasters and reputational issues. A few key components to include in your plan are:

- **Crisis Identification and Classification**: Define what constitutes a crisis and how to classify it (e.g., Minor,

Moderate, Major) based on potential impact.

- **Communication Protocols**: Outline how communication flows within the organization during a crisis, detailing who speaks to whom and how decisions are disseminated.

- **Notification Procedures**: Specify who needs to be notified, both internally (executives, employees) and externally (customers, media).

- **Stakeholder Mapping**: Identify key stakeholders for each type of crisis, including customers, regulators, media, and the community.

Creating this plan is not a one-and-done task. Regular updates and reviews are essential to ensure that the plan remains relevant, especially as the organization grows or shifts focus.

2. Conduct a Vulnerability Audit and Develop a Heat Map

A vulnerability audit is a comprehensive assessment of potential risks facing your organization. By identifying and evaluating these risks, you can pinpoint where your organization is most vulnerable and focus your crisis preparation efforts on those areas.

One effective tool for visualizing and prioritizing these risks is a heat map, which categorizes threats based on their likelihood and potential impact. For instance:

- **High Likelihood, High Impact**: Requires immediate attention and comprehensive crisis planning.

- **Low Likelihood, High Impact**: Needs contingency planning but may not require immediate action.

- **High Likelihood, Low Impact**: Often managed through existing protocols but should be included in regular monitoring.

- **Low Likelihood, Low Impact**: Minimal focus needed but should still be documented for thoroughness.

Completing a vulnerability audit and developing a heat map not only enhances your crisis readiness but also helps justify the allocation of resources and the importance of crisis planning to senior leadership.

3. Select and Train the Crisis Communications Management Team

A crisis response is only as effective as the team behind it. Selecting the Crisis Communications Management Team is a critical step in crisis preparation. The team should consist of individuals from key areas of the organization, as discussed in Chapter 2, including Communications, Marketing, Legal, Operations, Public Policy, and Human Resources. Each member should understand their specific role within the team, as well as the broader strategy for crisis response.

Training the Team:

- **Role-Specific Training**: Ensure each member knows their responsibilities and has the necessary skills to perform them under pressure.

- **Scenario-Based Exercises**: Conduct exercises that simulate realistic crisis scenarios, allowing team members to practice their response in a controlled environment.

- **Refresher Courses**: Crisis communication is a fast-evolving field, so regular training updates help the team stay sharp and informed about new best practices.

4. Develop, Test, and Maintain Facility Emergency Response and Disaster Recovery Plans

In addition to the Crisis Communications Plan, organizations should develop emergency response and disaster recovery plans for each facility. These plans address the immediate safety of personnel and assets, ensuring that the organization is prepared for events like natural disasters, fires, or on-site accidents.

Key Elements of Facility Plans:

- **Evacuation Routes and Safety Procedures**: Clearly defined evacuation routes, shelter-in-place procedures, and designated safety officers for each facility.
- **Disaster Recovery Processes**: Procedures for restoring critical operations, including data recovery and resuming production or services after a disruption.
- **Emergency Contacts**: Up-to-date contact lists for emergency services, utility providers, and on-site personnel with emergency management responsibilities.

Regularly testing and updating these plans is crucial, as outdated procedures can lead to confusion and potentially exacerbate the impact of a crisis.

5. Prepare and Maintain Global Contact Lists (Internal and External)

A fast response relies on efficient communication. Prepare and maintain comprehensive global contact lists that include internal team members, executives, and key external stakeholders. These lists should be organized and easily accessible in a crisis to facilitate rapid outreach.

Types of Contact Lists:
- **Internal Contacts**: Key executives, department heads,

crisis management team members, and other essential personnel.

- **External Contacts**: Customers, suppliers, regulatory bodies, media outlets, and emergency services.

- **Backup Contact Methods**: Ensure alternative contact methods are available (e.g., personal cell numbers, secondary email addresses) in case primary systems are disrupted.

6. Clarify and Communicate Roles and Responsibilities

Clear roles and responsibilities prevent confusion and streamline the response process. Documenting each team member's duties ensures that everyone knows their specific tasks, reducing the risk of duplication or oversight.

Roles to Define:

- **Decision Makers**: Who has the authority to make critical decisions under pressure?

- **Spokespersons**: Who will represent the organization publicly, and who will be the point of contact for media inquiries?

- **Internal Liaisons**: Who will communicate with employees and address internal concerns?

- **External Liaisons**: Who is responsible for managing relationships with customers, partners, and regulators?

Communicating these roles ahead of time gives team members the confidence to act decisively, ensuring a cohesive and effective response.

7. Conduct Crisis Communication Exercises

Finally, regular crisis communication exercises are essential to test the Crisis Communications Playbook and assess the team's readiness. These exercises simulate real crisis scenarios and help identify any weaknesses or gaps in the plan, allowing the team to refine its approach before an actual crisis occurs.

Types of Exercises:

- **Tabletop Exercises**: A discussion-based exercise where the team talks through their response to a simulated crisis scenario. Ideal for identifying gaps in communication protocols.

- **Full-Scale Drills**: A more immersive experience that involves the entire team and sometimes even external partners. These drills can reveal unforeseen challenges in coordination and logistics.

- **After-Action Reviews**: After each exercise, conduct a review to assess what went well, what didn't, and what changes are needed in the Crisis Communications Playbook.

THE ROI OF CRISIS PREPAREDNESS

Preparing for a crisis may seem like an investment with an uncertain return, but the costs of being unprepared are far higher. The time and resources spent on developing a crisis communications plan and training a capable team can prevent far greater losses in reputation, revenue, and customer trust if a crisis occurs.

Organizations that prioritize preparation through these pre-crisis steps not only safeguard their operations but also position themselves to navigate a crisis effectively, demonstrating to stakeholders that they are resilient and dependable—even in the toughest times.

Pre-Crisis Preparation Check List

1. **Establish a Crisis Communications Plan**
   - Define what constitutes a crisis and outline classification levels.
   - Set communication protocols and notification procedures.
   - Identify key stakeholders and assign primary and secondary contacts.

2. **Select and Train the Crisis Communications Team**

- Appoint leaders from Communications, Legal, HR, Operations, Public Policy, and other relevant departments.
- Train team members on crisis response, roles, and media handling.
- Conduct scenario-based exercises regularly.

3. **Conduct a Vulnerability Audit and Create a Heat Map**
    - Identify potential risks to the organization and prioritize them based on likelihood and impact.
        - Use a heat map to visualize vulnerabilities and allocate resources accordingly.

4. **Develop and Maintain Contact Lists**
    - Ensure up-to-date contact information for internal leaders, external stakeholders, media, regulators, and key partners.
        - Include alternative contact methods in case of system disruptions.

5. **Prepare Key Messaging Templates**
    - Draft templates for holding statements, press releases, social media updates, and internal communications.
    - Tailor messages for different crisis scenarios, audiences, and channels.

6. **Plan and Schedule Regular Crisis Drills**
    - Conduct tabletop exercises and full-scale simulations.
    - Include debriefing sessions to review performance and update the crisis plan as needed.

Key Takeaways:

1. **Preparation is Crucial**: Effective crisis management hinges on thorough preparation. Building a Crisis Communications Plan, conducting audits, training the team, and testing responses are foundational steps in preparing for a crisis before it occurs.

2. **Comprehensive Crisis Communications Plan**: A well-crafted Crisis Communications Plan serves as the backbone of an organization's crisis response. It includes crisis classification, communication protocols, notification procedures, and stakeholder mapping, all of which should be regularly updated to keep the plan relevant.

3. **Vulnerability Audit and Heat Mapping**: Conducting a vulnerability audit helps identify potential risks and allows organizations to prioritize their response efforts using a heat map. This tool categorizes risks based on their likelihood and impact, enabling a more focused allocation of resources.

4. **Training and Selecting the Crisis Communications Team**: A strong crisis response team should be cross-functional, comprising members from Communications, Legal, Operations, Marketing, Public Policy, and Human Resources. Regular scenario-based training ensures each team member understands their role and can perform under pressure.

5. **Facility Emergency and Disaster Recovery Plans**: Besides the overarching Crisis Communications Plan, each facility should have specific emergency response and disaster recovery plans. These plans cover evacuation routes, disaster recovery processes, and emergency contacts.

6. **Global Contact Lists**: Fast communication is essential in

a crisis. Maintaining up-to-date global contact lists for internal and external stakeholders ensures quick outreach. Backup contact methods should also be in place to handle system disruptions.

7. **Clear Roles and Responsibilities**: Assigning clear roles and responsibilities to team members helps prevent confusion and ensures a streamlined response. Knowing who the decision-makers, spokespersons, and liaisons are ahead of time allows for decisive action during a crisis.

8. **Crisis Communication Exercises**: Regular crisis communication exercises, including tabletop exercises and full-scale drills, test the Crisis Communications Playbook and identify areas for improvement. After-action reviews are essential to refine strategies based on exercise outcomes.

9. **Return on Investment of Preparedness**: Investing time and resources in crisis preparedness minimizes potential losses in reputation, revenue, and stakeholder trust when a crisis occurs. Prepared organizations demonstrate resilience and reliability, which strengthens stakeholder confidence.

Action Items:

1. **Develop and Regularly Update the Crisis Communications Plan**
   - Define what constitutes a crisis and establish classification levels (Minor, Moderate, Major).
   - Outline communication protocols and notification procedures.
   - Identify and map key stakeholders, ensuring primary and secondary contacts for each.

2. **Conduct a Vulnerability Audit and Create a Heat Map**
   - Assess potential risks to the organization, categorizing them by likelihood and impact.
   - Use a heat map to visualize and prioritize vulnerabilities, guiding resource allocation for crisis preparation.

3. **Appoint and Train the Crisis Communications Team**
   - Select leaders from relevant departments (Communications, Legal, Operations, etc.) to form the Crisis Communications Team.
   - Provide role-specific training and conduct regular scenario-based exercises to ensure readiness.
   - Schedule refresher courses and stay updated on crisis communication best practices.

4. **Create and Maintain Facility Emergency and Disaster Recovery Plans**
   - Develop site-specific emergency plans, including evacuation routes, disaster recovery protocols, and emergency contacts.
   - Test these plans regularly and update them as needed to reflect any operational or structural changes.

5. **Build and Maintain Comprehensive Contact Lists**

   - Prepare global contact lists with internal leaders, external stakeholders, regulatory bodies, and media outlets.
   - Ensure each contact has an alternative communication method (e.g., cell phone, secondary email) in case of disruptions.

6. **Draft Key Messaging Templates**

   - Prepare templates for holding statements, press releases, social media updates, and internal communications for various crisis scenarios.
   - Tailor these messages to different audiences (customers, employees, media) and channels to ensure quick, effective communication.

7. **Schedule Regular Crisis Communication Drills**

   - Conduct tabletop exercises for team discussions and full-scale simulations involving internal and external stakeholders.
   - Review each exercise through after-action reports, identifying areas for improvement and updating the Crisis Communications Playbook accordingly.

8. **Clarify and Communicate Team Roles and Responsibilities**

   - Define and document each team member's role, including decision-makers, spokespersons, internal and external liaisons.
   - Communicate these roles clearly within the team to foster confidence and ensure cohesive action when a crisis strikes.

By following these takeaways and action items, organizations can lay a strong foundation for crisis readiness, ensuring that they can respond swiftly, effectively, and empathetically to safeguard their operations, reputation, and stakeholder trust.

PART III: DURING THE CRISIS – RESPONDING WITH PRECISION AND CARE

In the midst of a crisis, every second counts. A well-prepared and strategically implemented response can save an organization's reputation, foster stakeholder trust, and minimize operational disruptions.

This section will explore the critical steps and best practices for responding to crises, including illustrative stories to emphasize the importance of timing, accuracy, and empathy. Through real-world scenarios and detailed frameworks, we'll delve into the mechanics of effective crisis communication.

A Tale of Two Brands: Speed and Clarity in Action

In the spring of 2020, two food brands found themselves facing an identical crisis: potential product contamination that led to a recall.

Brand A, with a solid crisis communications plan, quickly mobilized its team and issued a holding statement within ten minutes, followed by a comprehensive public response within an hour. Their messaging was clear, transparent, and empathic, with a focus on customer safety and actionable steps.

Brand B, in contrast, had no established plan and delayed its response to verify information. Their first public statement came out the next day, vague and uncertain, allowing rumors to spiral and frustration to grow.

By the time Brand B issued a clear message, trust was eroded, and customers had already turned to social media to vent. In the end, Brand A's swift response preserved its reputation and even strengthened customer loyalty, while Brand B suffered lasting reputational damage.

The lesson is clear: a quick, accurate, and consistent response is essential. This principle will guide the strategies and actions explored in this section.

CORE PRINCIPLES OF CRISIS COMMUNICATION: BE QUICK, BE ACCURATE, BE CONSISTENT

An effective crisis response revolves around three core principles:

1. **Be Quick**: Speed is essential in crisis management. The organization's promptness in acknowledging and addressing the situation can prevent the spread of misinformation and reassure stakeholders.

2. **Be Accurate**: Facts matter. Communicating with errors or speculation can damage credibility. All information shared should be verified to prevent the need for retractions.

3. **Be Consistent**: With multiple departments and spokespeople involved, consistency is key. Coordinated messaging across all channels prevents confusion and reinforces trust.

These principles serve as a compass, guiding the Crisis Communications Team to respond with precision and clarity.

ASSESSING THE CRISIS: THE FOUNDATION OF AN EFFECTIVE RESPONSE

When a crisis unfolds, the initial response should begin with a comprehensive assessment. This assessment allows the Core Crisis Management Team to gauge the severity of the incident, anticipate potential outcomes, and mobilize resources effectively.

Below is a structured approach for evaluating a crisis, focusing on ten key areas of inquiry.

Preliminary Analysis: Setting the Stage

An initial assessment provides the foundation for a tailored crisis response. The following questions guide the team in understanding the scope, intensity, and potential consequences of the situation:

1. **Scope and Probability of the Problem**
   - **Key Questions**: What is the scope of the issue (local, regional, national, global)? Is it theoretical or ongoing? What is the likelihood of immediate impact?
   - **Explanation**: Understanding the scale helps allocate

resources proportionately, ensuring an appropriate response.

2. **Level of Intensity and Escalation Potential**
   - **Key Questions**: What is the current intensity? Could it escalate?
   - **Explanation**: A small issue might be manageable within existing protocols, but if there's potential for escalation, the response must adapt accordingly.

3. **Impact on Employees and Public Safety**
   - **Key Questions**: Does the crisis pose a direct threat to safety? Are safety protocols necessary?
   - **Explanation**: Prioritizing safety mitigates legal and reputational risks. Safety-first measures are essential for any crisis response involving potential harm.

4. **Operational Impact**
   - **Key Questions**: How does this affect business operations? Will there be significant disruptions?
   - **Explanation**: A thorough understanding of operational impact enables proactive management of productivity and service continuity.

5. **Reputational Impact**
   - **Key Questions**: Could this crisis damage the organization's reputation? How might stakeholders view the incident?
   - **Explanation**: Reputation is a valuable asset. A proactive approach to public perception can help mitigate potential reputational harm.

6. **Media Interest**
   - **Key Questions**: Is the media aware of the crisis? How likely is it that they will cover it?
   - **Explanation**: Preparing for media attention allows

the organization to control the narrative and avoid unexpected scrutiny.

7. **Regulatory and Policy Considerations**
   - **Key Questions**: Does this crisis fall under any regulatory obligations? Are compliance reports required?
   - **Explanation**: Ensuring regulatory compliance prevents potential legal repercussions.

8. **Financial Impact**
   - **Key Questions**: What is the potential financial impact?
   - **Explanation**: Estimating financial repercussions is essential for maintaining transparency with investors and preparing for budget adjustments.

9. **Competitive Landscape**
   - **Key Questions**: Are competitors aware, or likely to leverage the situation?
   - **Explanation**: Competitors may use the crisis to their advantage. The organization should strategize to maintain its market position.

10. **Legal Implications**
    - **Key Questions**: Are there potential legal consequences, such as lawsuits or compliance violations?
    - **Explanation**: Identifying legal risks early allows the team to work closely with legal advisors, ensuring compliance and minimizing liability.

Using this checklist, the Core Crisis Management Team can evaluate the severity of the crisis, assign a crisis level, and coordinate an appropriate response.

CRISIS CLASSIFICATION SYSTEM - ASSESSING AND ESCALATING RISK

In the heat of a crisis, determining the level of severity and deciding on the appropriate response is essential to protecting an organization's operations, reputation, and people.

The Crisis Classification System provides a structured approach to evaluate crises and assign them a level, from minor to major, based on their potential impact. This system guides the Core Crisis Communications Team in assessing the situation, escalating if necessary, and mobilizing resources effectively.

Crises are rarely static. As new information comes to light, the severity of a situation may increase or decrease. This chapter introduces a crisis rating framework, outlining each level and the key factors to consider for effective classification. When in doubt, it's always safer to escalate—a minor response to a major risk can have far-reaching consequences.

Key Takeaways:

1. **The Three Core Principles of Crisis Communication**:

- **Be Quick**: Speed is crucial in crisis communication. Responding quickly prevents misinformation and reassures stakeholders that the organization is actively addressing the situation.
- **Be Accurate**: Accuracy builds trust. All shared

information should be verified to avoid retractions, which can damage credibility.

- **Be Consistent**: Consistency across all departments and spokespeople is essential. Coordinated messaging prevents confusion, reinforces trust, and protects the organization's reputation.

2. **Importance of Initial Crisis Assessment**: A thorough assessment of the crisis allows the Core Crisis Management Team to gauge the severity and potential outcomes, enabling them to allocate resources effectively. This step sets the stage for a tailored response that addresses the crisis's specific needs.

3. **Ten Key Areas for Crisis Assessment**: By examining ten critical areas—scope, intensity, safety, operational impact, reputation, media interest, regulatory considerations, financial impact, competitive landscape, and legal implications—the team can form a comprehensive understanding of the crisis and determine the best course of action.

4. **Crisis Classification System**: The Crisis Classification System categorizes crises based on severity, allowing the organization to respond proportionately. The system guides the escalation process, ensuring that resources and communication strategies match the crisis's level of impact.

5. **Proactive Escalation**: Since crises are dynamic, the organization should regularly reassess and be ready to escalate its response if new information suggests heightened severity. Escalating early rather than underestimating can prevent larger consequences.

Action Items:

1. **Apply the Core Principles in All Crisis Responses**:
   - **Respond Quickly**: Ensure that the Crisis Communications Team is prepared to issue a holding statement immediately, with a comprehensive update to follow.
   - **Verify All Information Before Release**: Implement a system for fact-checking all messages to avoid mistakes or misstatements.
   - **Coordinate Messaging Across Teams**: Schedule regular alignment meetings with all departments involved in the crisis response to ensure consistent communication.

2. **Conduct a Comprehensive Initial Crisis Assessment**:

- Use the ten key areas of inquiry (scope, intensity, safety, etc.) as a checklist to guide the Core Crisis Management Team's assessment of each crisis.
- Regularly revisit and update this assessment as new details emerge, ensuring that the response evolves with the crisis.

3. **Classify the Crisis Using the Crisis Classification System**:

- Assign a crisis level (e.g., Minor, Moderate, Major) based on initial assessment findings, determining the required resources and response urgency.
- Err on the side of caution if the severity is uncertain, opting for a higher classification level to ensure adequate resource allocation.

4. **Create a Crisis Escalation Protocol**:

- Establish a clear protocol for escalating a crisis based on specific triggers, such as increased media interest or new safety concerns.
- Implement a process for ongoing monitoring and reassessment to capture any shifts in crisis severity, enabling the organization to respond with agility.

5. **Prepare for Media Attention and Public Scrutiny**:

- Monitor social and traditional media for mentions of the crisis, allowing the team to gauge public sentiment and media interest.
- Prepare media statements in advance for high-risk scenarios, ensuring the organization is ready to address potential scrutiny with factual, consistent messaging.

6. **Document and Review Each Crisis for Continuous Improvement**:

- After the crisis, document the response process, including any issues encountered, lessons learned, and adjustments made in real-time.
- Use these insights to refine the Crisis Classification System and response protocols, improving preparedness for future crises.

By adhering to these takeaways and action items, organizations can ensure a swift, accurate, and consistent crisis response that protects their operations, reputation, and stakeholder trust.

The Escalation Decision

Nightmare at NovaTech

I t was a quiet Wednesday morning when *NovaTech Manufacturing* received a troubling call from one of its warehouse managers. A minor electrical fire had broken out overnight, causing some localized smoke damage but no injuries. The incident seemed contained and limited, and the team classified it as a Level 1 - Minor Risk. They assumed the situation could be handled through normal departmental processes.

However, as the day progressed, more details emerged. The fire had affected a section of the warehouse that housed critical components for a top client's product, and due to the smoke damage, these parts would have to be discarded. Even worse, the warehouse had been storing a backlog of shipments due to recent supply chain delays, so the loss was greater than initially estimated. As suppliers and customers began contacting NovaTech for updates, the company quickly realized this wasn't just a minor issue.

By mid-morning, NovaTech's Core Crisis Management Team re-evaluated the situation. Recognizing the broader impact on customers and the potential for media coverage if supply chain delays were prolonged, they decided to reclassify the crisis to Level 2 - Moderate Risk. Within hours, the team had notified the Crisis Communications team, activated a broader response plan, and informed affected clients about potential delays.

NovaTech's experience highlights the importance of flexibility and escalation in crisis classification. A Level 1 crisis can quickly escalate, and by staying vigilant and reassessing the situation, NovaTech was able to mitigate a larger reputational hit and keep clients informed.

I. UNDERSTANDING THE CRISIS CLASSIFICATION LEVELS

The Crisis Classification System categorizes crises into three levels based on the scope, impact, and urgency of the situation. This framework allows organizations to respond in a manner proportionate to the crisis, ensuring that resources and attention are aligned with the severity of the issue.

Level 1 - Minor Risk

Definition: Minor impact confined to:

- A single facility
- A very limited number of customers, suppliers, or community members

Characteristics:

- Does not involve regulatory, customer, or authority concerns.
- Unlikely to attract media attention.
- Managed through regular departmental processes without major disruption.

Scope:

- One-time event, such as a minor business problem or local incident (e.g., minor equipment failure, isolated customer complaint).
- Impact is localized and can be controlled without affecting the broader organization.

Business and Financial Impact:

- Temporary, with business operations likely to return to normal within a few days.
- Minimal financial impact, primarily confined to operational areas.

Customer Impact:

- No direct impact on customers, and no special communication required beyond standard procedures.

Competitive Impact:

- Minimal risk, as the issue is contained internally and unlikely to be exploited by competitors.

Judicial/Regulatory Impact:

- Little to no chance of legal or regulatory action. Minor compliance reporting may be required.

Examples:

- Product defect affecting a limited area, but no significant health risk.
- Localized labor issue with minimal disruption.
- Supply chain issue contained within a single facility.

Level 2 - Moderate Risk

Definition: Limited impact to:

- Day-to-day activities or operations, affecting multiple stakeholders.
- Includes challenges in production or delivery but

manageable with coordinated effort.

Characteristics:

- Temporary disruption, with operations expected to resume within 30 days.
- May attract some media coverage and requires notification to the Crisis Communications team.

Scope:

- Serious disruption impacting company facilities, employees, or stakeholders for a limited time.
- May escalate if not managed effectively or if public perception worsens.

Business and Financial Impact:

- Moderate financial impact, possibly requiring additional resources to manage the crisis.
- Temporary shutdown or closure of facilities, inventory shortages, or supply chain delays.

Customer Impact: Likely to prompt concerns from customers; proactive communication is recommended once the situation is resolved.

Competitive Impact: Opportunity for competitors to leverage the situation if it gains public attention, potentially impacting market share.

Judicial/Regulatory Impact: Possible lawsuits or regulatory inquiries, especially if the situation has public health or safety implications.

Examples:

- Fire, chemical spill, or explosion with limited property damage but no injuries.
- Litigation, such as product liability claims or patent infringement disputes.
- Moderate product recall that may temporarily affect

customer access to products.

Level 3 - Major Risk

Definition: Severe impact to: Business activities, one or more facilities, the ability to produce or deliver products, and the company's financial standing or reputation.

Characteristics:

- Long-term business interruption and significant potential for ongoing media coverage.
- Requires immediate activation of the Crisis Communications team and executive leadership involvement.

Scope:

- Highly disruptive situation affecting the entire organization, its reputation, and its financial outcomes.
- Expected to have an indefinite impact if not managed effectively.

Business and Financial Impact:

- Substantial financial damage with potential long-term consequences on sales and operational viability.
- Operations and day-to-day activities are disrupted for an extended period.

Customer Impact: Customers may receive defective products or face extended delays, potentially resulting in loss of market share.

Competitive Impact: Significant threat to competitive standing, as competitors may capitalize on the crisis or attract dissatisfied customers.

Judicial/Regulatory Impact: High likelihood of regulatory involvement, lawsuits, or class actions, especially if public health and safety are compromised.

Examples:

- Large-scale chemical spill, fire, explosion, or natural disaster with major damage, injuries, or fatalities.
- Product recall linked to severe health risks or major disruptions to customer access.
- Loss of key executive(s) in an accident, resulting in leadership void.

II. Crisis Classification System in Practice

The Crisis Classification System offers a structured way to evaluate a crisis based on its initial impact, with each level guiding the organization's response.

However, classification should remain flexible. As seen in the NovaTech Manufacturing example, a minor issue can escalate quickly, necessitating re-evaluation and, if needed, escalation to a higher crisis level.

When in Doubt, Escalate: If the severity of a crisis is unclear or if it seems to fall between two levels, err on the side of caution. Classifying a crisis at a higher level ensures that resources and attention are sufficient to manage the potential impact.

Regular Reassessment: As more information becomes available, the Core Crisis Management Team should reassess the classification to determine if escalation or de-escalation is warranted. This ongoing assessment is crucial for effective response management.

III. Key Factors to Consider in Crisis Classification

When classifying a crisis, consider the following factors to determine the appropriate level:

1. **Scope of the Situation**: Evaluate the geographic reach, scale, and duration of the impact. A localized issue might be manageable as a Level 1 crisis, while a widespread disruption across multiple facilities would likely require escalation.

2. **Business and Financial Impact**: Assess the effect on day-to-day operations and long-term financial health. Short-term losses may align with Level 1 or Level 2, but significant operational challenges, such as plant closures or product recalls, may indicate a Level 3 crisis.

3. **Customer and Stakeholder Reactions**: Gauge the level of customer concern or outrage, as well as the potential for stakeholder inquiries. A crisis that directly affects customer access or product quality will often require a higher classification.

4. **Media and Public Sentiment**: Analyze media coverage and public reactions. Viral social media attention can quickly elevate a situation from a minor issue to a major reputational risk. **Research from Edelman** reveals that **25% of viral crisis content** originates from public reaction, underscoring the importance of monitoring public sentiment.

5. **Regulatory or Legal Implications**: Consider the likelihood of regulatory inquiries, lawsuits, or class actions. A crisis that raises safety or compliance concerns often requires a higher level of response.

IV. Using the Classification System to Guide Response

The Crisis Classification System is a powerful tool that allows organizations to respond proportionately to the severity of each crisis.

By assessing scope, financial impact, customer reactions, and regulatory implications, the organization can deploy appropriate resources, notify key teams, and execute an effective communication strategy.

As crises evolve, so too must the organization's approach. Flexibility, vigilance, and a willingness to escalate when in doubt are essential to protecting the organization's operations, reputation, and people during times of crisis.

Key Takeaways:

1. **Crisis Classification Levels**: Crises are categorized into three levels—Minor, Moderate, and Major—based on scope, impact, and urgency. This system ensures the organization's response is proportionate to the crisis severity, optimizing resource allocation and minimizing disruption.

   - **Level 1 - Minor Risk**: Confined impact, managed through departmental processes, and unlikely to attract media attention or regulatory concerns.

   - **Level 2 - Moderate Risk**: Wider impact with potential media interest, requiring coordinated efforts and proactive communication with stakeholders.

   - **Level 3 - Major Risk**: Severe, organization-wide impact with high potential for financial and reputational damage, demanding immediate involvement of executive leadership and the Crisis Communications team.

2. **Crisis Classification in Practice**: The classification system provides a structured approach to evaluate a crisis and assign it an appropriate response level. However, flexibility is essential, as a crisis may escalate, requiring re-evaluation and reclassification.

3. **Escalate When in Doubt**: When the severity is unclear or the crisis falls between two levels, it's best to classify it at the higher level. This approach ensures sufficient resources and attention are allocated to manage the potential impact effectively.

4. **Regular Reassessment**: Crisis situations can evolve, and continuous reassessment is critical. As new information emerges, the crisis level may need to be adjusted, either up or down, to align the response with the current reality.

5. **Key Factors in Crisis Classification**: Five primary factors—scope, business and financial impact, customer and stakeholder reactions, media/public sentiment, and regulatory/legal implications—provide a comprehensive framework for classifying crises and tailoring the response accordingly.

6. **Guided, Proportional Response**: The Crisis Classification System enables organizations to deploy resources and craft responses in proportion to the severity of the crisis, balancing the need for swift action with appropriate resource use.

Action Items:

1. **Implement the Crisis Classification System**
   - Integrate the three crisis levels (Minor, Moderate, Major) into the organization's crisis response framework.
   - Train team members on the characteristics of each level to ensure accurate initial classification when a crisis occurs.

2. **Prepare for Escalation Protocols**
   - Establish clear guidelines for when and how to escalate a crisis to a higher level if new information suggests increased severity.
   - Develop contingency plans for each level to facilitate quick adaptation if reclassification becomes necessary.

3. **Conduct Regular Reassessments**
   - Schedule routine check-ins during a crisis to re-evaluate its classification as more information becomes available.
   - Ensure the Core Crisis Management Team monitors the crisis's development and adjusts the response level as needed.

4. **Evaluate Key Crisis Factors During Classification**
   - Use the five key factors—scope, financial impact, customer reactions, media sentiment, and regulatory implications—to guide classification decisions.
   - Document each factor's influence on the crisis level to improve consistency in decision-making across different crises.

5. **Engage in Media and Public Sentiment Monitoring**
   - Implement tools to monitor social media, news outlets, and public sentiment. Proactive monitoring helps detect shifts in public perception that may require an escalation in response level.

- Assign a team member to track sentiment and report trends, allowing the organization to stay ahead of potential reputational impacts.

6. **Develop Crisis Scenarios for Training and Simulations**

   - Create crisis simulation exercises that cover each classification level to help the team practice identifying, classifying, and escalating crises in real-time.
   - Use these exercises to train the Crisis Communications and Core Crisis Management Teams in applying the classification system accurately.

7. **Document Lessons from Real Crises**

   - After each crisis, review and document how the classification level was determined and adjusted throughout the response.
   - Analyze the effectiveness of the chosen classification and response strategy, noting any lessons that can improve future crisis management efforts.

By following these takeaways and action items, organizations can ensure that their response is appropriately scaled to each crisis's severity, maintaining operational continuity, protecting reputation, and preserving stakeholder trust.

Initial Crisis Response Actions:
From Holding Statements to Full Transparency

An organization's response in the first hour of a crisis can determine how effectively it manages the entire situation. Immediate actions, such as issuing a holding statement, ensuring accurate messaging, and designating a spokesperson, are essential to establishing control and fostering trust.

Step-by-Step Guide to the Initial Response:

1. **Issue a Holding Statement (within 10 Minutes)**
   - Acknowledge the issue without providing unverified details, assuring stakeholders that the organization is aware and taking action.
   - **Example**: "We are aware of the situation involving [specifics] and are currently assessing its impact. Our top priority is the safety and well-being of all affected. We will provide more information as soon as it becomes available."

2. **Release an Initial Response (within 60 Minutes)**
   - Share a comprehensive response with verified information, outlining immediate actions and addressing public concerns.
   - **Example**: "After thoroughly reviewing the situation, we have taken steps to ensure [specific safety measures, actions taken]. Our teams are actively working to resolve this issue, and we will continue to provide updates."

3. **Identify a Spokesperson**
   - Choose a spokesperson with credibility, ideally a high-ranking official like a Vice President or the CEO. Equip them with key messages, Q&A, and talking points.
   - **Tip**: Ensure the spokesperson is prepared to address difficult questions calmly and confidently to convey control and professionalism.

4. **Gather Essential Information and Prepare Responses**
   1. Collect details on what happened, when, who is affected, and the potential impacts. Prepare responses for media and stakeholders.
   2. **Explanation**: Information gathering helps shape an accurate narrative and avoid the spread of misinformation.

5. **Prioritize Communication Channels and Audience-**

Specific Messaging

- Use multiple communication channels, from social media to email, to reach various stakeholders.

- **Explanation**: Consistent and targeted messaging ensures all audiences receive relevant and timely information.

CASE STUDY: PRIORITIZING SAFETY AND EMPATHY

In 2019, a popular toy company faced a recall crisis when it was discovered that a specific product contained a hazardous material. They immediately issued a holding statement and instructed parents to stop using the product. The CEO addressed the public in a video statement, expressing genuine concern and outlining the company's recall process.

In addition to explaining the recall steps, the company offered refunds and set up a hotline for parents. This empathetic approach helped mitigate backlash, and within weeks, the company had regained customer trust, with many parents applauding the company's transparency and quick action.

The lesson? Prioritizing safety and empathy can turn a potentially disastrous situation into an opportunity to build loyalty.

MAINTAINING A CALM, RATIONAL TONE

During a crisis, emotions run high, and the tone of communication plays a crucial role in managing public perception. Striking a calm, rational tone conveys control and confidence.

Avoid Downplaying or Sensationalizing: Downplaying may come across as indifferent, while sensationalizing can incite unnecessary panic. Find a balanced, measured approach.

Set a Reassuring Tone: Confidence and composure in messaging help prevent fear and confusion. For instance, emphasizing actionable steps taken to address the crisis reassures stakeholders that the situation is under control.

Example Scenario: In 2021, a pharmaceutical company experienced a minor production delay due to a temporary shortage of materials. Instead of downplaying the issue, they acknowledged the delay and reassured patients, explaining that they were working to resolve the issue quickly. This transparent approach minimized panic and maintained trust.

GATHERING INFORMATION – PREPARING FOR CRISIS COMMUNICATION

In the midst of a crisis, having accurate, comprehensive information is the backbone of effective communication. The details of what happened, who is affected, and what steps are being taken will shape the organization's messages to the public, stakeholders, and media.

During a crisis, media inquiries will come swiftly, often covering sensitive topics, and responses need to be well-prepared and precise.

Gathering information is not just about answering questions—it's about understanding the situation in its entirety. Each question posed by the media or stakeholders provides an opportunity to shape the narrative and reinforce trust. The following sections cover key topics for gathering information, including business-related questions, product defects, restructuring, labor disputes, disaster responses, and managing rumors.

I. BUSINESS-RELATED QUESTIONS

In most crises, there are foundational questions that media, stakeholders, and the public will want answered. These questions help clarify what happened and the immediate impact on the organization, its customers, and the community.

Key Questions to Prepare For:
- **What happened?** Provide a clear, factual account of the incident.
- **When did it happen?** Detail the timeline to show transparency.
- **Who is involved?** Identify affected parties, from employees to external partners.
- **Were we aware of any problems beforehand?** If applicable, explain what was known and any proactive measures taken.
- **What led to the problem?** Avoid speculation but give context for the root cause if known.
- **What is the impact on customers/patients/donors/ community?** Outline how they may be affected and any assistance being provided.
- **What authorities need to be notified and when?** Explain compliance with regulatory requirements.
- **Have we informed the relevant authorities?** Reassure that

proper procedures have been followed.

- **What is the financial impact?** Disclose potential financial repercussions, if appropriate.
- **What is the impact to productivity/service?** Clarify if there will be any service disruptions or delays.
- **Do we need to shut down temporarily?** Provide details if operations are suspended or affected.
- **When will we reopen?** If closed, set expectations for resuming normal business.

These questions are fundamental and should be answered in a factual, concise manner, ensuring transparency and reassuring stakeholders of the organization's commitment to managing the situation effectively.

II. Restructure or New Business Model

Restructuring, layoffs, or business model changes can provoke concern and anxiety among employees, stakeholders, and the public. Preparing responses to questions about these changes can help control the narrative and reassure stakeholders about the organization's future.

Key Questions to Prepare For:

- **Will there be any staff reductions? How many?** Be specific and transparent about any layoffs, if applicable.
- **What is the current total number of staff?** Provide context for the scale of the restructuring.
- **Will there be more layoffs in the near future?** Offer clarity about future staffing plans, if possible.
- **Why are you doing this?** Explain the rationale behind the restructuring, focusing on long-term benefits.
- **How did we decide how many staff to lay off?** Detail the

process to show it was thoughtful and necessary.

Addressing these questions with empathy and transparency is essential, as restructuring affects employees and can impact morale and public perception.

III. Product Defects

Product defects, especially those impacting consumer safety, demand a clear, reassuring response. Safety and quality con
trol are critical, and any issues in these areas can quickly damage trust.

Key Questions to Prepare For:

- **What exactly is wrong with the product?** Explain the defect in plain terms.
- **Were you aware of any problems before distribution?** Address what was known and what quality controls were in place.
- **Have any fatalities occurred?** Be honest but sensitive; clarify if there is any threat to life.
- **Will you pay compensation to affected customers?** Outline compensation plans if applicable.
- **How could this have happened?** Describe what went wrong without speculation.
- **When did you discover the problem?** Provide a timeline to show prompt response.
- **How many products are affected?** Give an accurate count if possible.
- **Have you stopped production?** Reassure stakeholders that steps are being taken to prevent further issues.
- **Have relevant authorities been notified?** Confirm compliance with legal and regulatory requirements.

- **Has this happened before?** Address any similar incidents and changes implemented since.
- **Will you review quality control procedures?** Reassure the public that improvements are being made.

Product defects can impact company profits, sales, and reputation, so clear and proactive communication is essential to regain trust.

IV. Disputes and Labor Issues

Labor disputes and other workplace conflicts can disrupt operations and attract public scrutiny. Preparing responses that show respect for employee concerns while protecting the company's interests is crucial.

Key Questions to Prepare For:

- **What is the dispute about?** Describe the issue concisely and factually.
- **Why are you not meeting their demands?** Offer the organization's perspective and rationale.
- **Will you terminate employees who do not return to work?** Be transparent about policies and potential outcomes.
- **Are you in discussion with the aggrieved employees?** Reassure that the company is open to resolution.
- **How many are affected by this labor dispute?** Provide numbers to give context.
- **How will you ensure there is no inconvenience to customers?** Explain measures taken to minimize disruptions.

Disputes can affect the organization's reputation and operations, so responses should convey a commitment to resolving the issue fairly.

V. DISASTER-RELATED CRISES

Natural or man-made disasters demand immediate, compassionate responses. Safety and recovery efforts are the primary focus, but accurate information and transparency are also critical.

Key Questions to Prepare For:

- **What happened?** Offer a concise, clear account of the incident.
- **When did it happen?** Provide a timeline for the event.
- **Have you identified the cause?** Avoid speculation but share known facts.
- **Were you aware of any problem beforehand?** Address preventive measures, if any.
- **Are there casualties or fatalities?** Confirm with sensitivity, acknowledging the impact on families and the community.
- **Will you be paying compensation?** Provide details on any assistance or compensation for affected individuals.

In disaster scenarios, empathetic communication and prioritizing safety are crucial to maintaining public trust.

VI. Managing Rumors

Rumors can create significant challenges during a crisis, as speculation can easily escalate and become a distraction. Knowing which topics to address and which to avoid is essential in rumor control.

General Stance on Rumor Response:

- **Acquisitions, Dispositions**: Generally, do not confirm or deny business dealings such as acquisitions or joint ventures unless there is a compelling reason.
- **Activities of Other Companies**: Avoid commenting on the actions of other companies.
- **Rumors of Layoffs or Closures**: Typically, do not comment on speculations about layoffs or closures.
- **Geopolitical Events or Foreign Affairs**: Direct such inquiries to experts or appropriate authorities.
- **Quarterly/Annual Financial Performance**: Avoid discussing financial predictions outside of official reports.
- **Security Programs**: Do not disclose security measures that could compromise safety.
- **Travel Plans of Senior Executives**: Do not discuss executive travel plans for security reasons.
- **Supplier or Vendor Relations**: Avoid commenting on specific suppliers unless directly relevant to the crisis.
- **Speculation or Predictions**: In general, avoid engaging in speculation.

In most cases, the organization's response to rumors should be brief and neutral, redirecting focus to verified facts rather than engaging in or validating speculation.

PREPARING RESPONSES FOR PUBLIC AND INTERNAL COMMUNICATION

As information is gathered, the Crisis Communications Team must organize and prioritize responses to address each key area of inquiry. Not all answers will be publicly shared, and some details may be reserved for internal communications or regulatory bodies.

Tailoring responses with careful consideration of each audience's needs helps to maintain transparency without oversharing or escalating concerns.

Creating Key Messages and Q&A:
- **Key Messages**: Identify core messages that reinforce the organization's values, empathy, and commitment to resolution.
- **Holding Statements**: Prepare initial statements for immediate release, especially if media is already aware of the situation.
- **Q&A Documents**: Develop a question-and-answer document to support spokespersons in addressing specific

inquiries concisely and accurately.

Proactive Social Listening: Monitor social media and public sentiment to identify emerging concerns or misinformation that may need addressing. Social listening helps the Crisis Communications Team stay ahead of rumors and adjust messaging in real time.

CLOSING THOUGHTS ON GATHERING INFORMATION

Effective crisis communication begins with accurate, thorough information gathering. By anticipating media questions and proactively preparing responses, the Crisis Communications Team can manage the flow of information and maintain control over the narrative.

In this way, the organization can reassure stakeholders, mitigate reputational damage, and emerge from the crisis with trust and credibility intact.

CRISIS COMMUNICATION STRATEGIES: THE BENEFITS OF EFFECTIVE MANAGEMENT

Effective crisis communication isn't just about damage control; it's about fostering trust and building resilience.

Studies show that organizations with strong crisis communication plans recover more quickly and maintain higher customer loyalty. The key benefits of a well-executed crisis response include:

1. **Faster Recovery**: Organizations with crisis communication plans recover 40% faster than those without.
2. **Customer Loyalty**: 82% of consumers are more likely to trust brands that handle crises well, according to McKinsey & Company.

3. **Reputational Resilience**: A swift, transparent response minimizes reputational damage, ensuring the organization can regain trust.

By handling crises effectively, organizations can emerge not only intact but also strengthened.

IMPLEMENTING THE CRISIS RESPONSE: A COORDINATED TEAM EFFORT

The Core Crisis Management Team and Crisis Communications Team must work in tandem to manage each aspect of the response.

Clear roles and consistent updates ensure that all team members are aligned and informed.

1. **Regular Updates and Briefings**
    - Frequent updates help the Communications Team maintain accuracy and timeliness.
2. **Clear Delegation of Responsibilities**
    - Each team member should understand their specific role to prevent duplication and ensure efficiency.

3. **Consistent Messaging**
    - Coordinated communication ensures all messages,

internal and external, align with the organization's response strategy.

This unified approach helps streamline operations, allowing the organization to respond efficiently and effectively.

CRISIS COMMUNICATIONS RESPONSE PLAN AND PROCESS: A STEP-BY-STEP FRAMEWORK

1. **Activate Plan and Initiate Response**: Get the crisis plan up and running, gathering personnel and issuing initial instructions.

2. **Assess the Situation**: Review crisis details, assign a risk level, and convene the Crisis Communications Team.

3. **Identify Spokesperson**: Choose a qualified spokesperson and provide them with key messages.

4. **Gather Information**: Monitor crisis developments, verify information, and refine messaging.

5. **Communicate Often**: Provide clear messages, monitor responses, and keep stakeholders informed.

6. **Refine Strategy and Continue Communications**: Adjust the response as new information emerges.

7. **Close the Crisis**: Conclude crisis operations while

addressing any lingering concerns.

8. **Analyze the Response**: Review strengths and areas for improvement, integrating insights into future planning.

Building Trust and Resilience Through

Crisis Communication

A structured crisis response is essential to managing communication effectively in turbulent times. By following a well-coordinated approach, the organization can respond decisively, keep stakeholders informed, and protect its reputation.

Consistent evaluation and updates to the crisis plan ensure that each experience strengthens the organization's readiness and resilience, preparing it to face future challenges with confidence and clarity.

During Crisis Response Check List

1. **Activate the Crisis Communications Plan**
   - Assemble the Crisis Management and Communications teams.
   - Convene an initial response meeting to assess the situation and set immediate goals.

2. **Assess the Situation**
   - Determine the crisis level (Minor, Moderate, or Major) based on scope, impact, and severity.
   - Confirm facts and avoid speculation; monitor the situation continuously.

3. **Identify a Spokesperson**
   - Select an appropriate spokesperson based on the nature of the crisis (e.g., CEO for major crises).

- Brief the spokesperson with approved key messages, Q&A, and talking points.

4. **Gather Essential Information**
   - Document what happened, who is affected, when it occurred, and where.
   - Identify root causes, assess financial impacts, and notify relevant authorities.
   - Monitor social media and news coverage for emerging narratives.

5. **Develop Key Messages and Communication Materials**
   - Use the "Be Quick, Be Accurate, Be Consistent" principle.
   - Prepare holding statements within 10 minutes and a full response within 60 minutes.
   - Customize messages for each audience: customers, employees, media, and stakeholders.

6. **Communicate Regularly and Transparently**
   - Provide updates as new information becomes available; avoid long silences.
   - Address rumors and misinformation through proactive social listening and fact-checking.
   - Tailor messaging for different platforms (e.g., social media, press releases, emails).

7. **Prioritize Safety and Empathy**
   - Make safety the primary concern; provide clear instructions for employees and affected parties.
   - Express empathy and offer support to those impacted, including compensation or resources if needed.

8. **Monitor Media and Public Sentiment**
   - Track news coverage and social media for tone and accuracy.
   - Respond to inaccuracies quickly and be prepared to adjust messaging as the crisis unfolds.

9. **Keep Internal Stakeholders Informed**
   - Update executives and department heads regularly on the crisis response and key developments.
   - Communicate with employees, providing reassurance and instructions as needed.

Key Takeaways:

1. **Swift Initial Response Sets the Tone for Crisis Management**: The first hour of a crisis is crucial for establishing control. Immediate actions like issuing a holding statement, preparing accurate messaging, and identifying a spokesperson are vital to prevent misinformation and reassure stakeholders.

2. **Accuracy, Transparency, and Consistency Build Credibility**: The principles of being quick, accurate, and consistent guide every aspect of the crisis response. Verified information and regular updates maintain trust, while consistency across channels avoids confusion and reinforces the organization's commitment to transparency.

3. **Empathy and Safety Are Priorities**: Prioritizing the safety and well-being of those affected and addressing concerns with empathy can help mitigate backlash. This approach builds goodwill, as seen in case studies where companies regained trust by showing genuine concern and proactive communication.

4. **Comprehensive Information Gathering Shapes Effective Communication**: Gathering accurate details about the incident, its impact, and response measures is essential. This helps create a well-informed narrative that reassures stakeholders and mitigates rumors or misinformation.

5. **Tailored Messaging for Different Audiences Enhances Communication Effectiveness**: Using audience-specific messages and multiple channels ensures that all stakeholders receive relevant, timely information, whether they are customers, employees, or media.

6. **Monitoring Media and Social Sentiment Is Critical for Reputation Management**: Proactive monitoring of media

and public sentiment helps the organization stay ahead of the narrative, address inaccuracies quickly, and adjust the response as the situation evolves.

7. **A Coordinated Crisis Team Improves Response Efficiency**: The Crisis Management and Communications teams must work in tandem to manage both operational and communicative aspects of the crisis. Regular updates, role clarity, and consistent messaging are essential for a unified, effective response.

Action Items:

1. **Issue a Holding Statement Within 10 Minutes**
   - Prepare a brief statement acknowledging awareness of the situation without speculating or offering unverified details.
   - Example: "We are aware of the situation and are actively assessing its impact. Our priority is the safety and well-being of all affected. We will provide more information as soon as it becomes available."

2. **Release an Initial Response Within 60 Minutes**
   - Share verified information with the public, addressing immediate actions and reassuring stakeholders.
   - **Example:** "After thoroughly reviewing the situation, we have taken steps to ensure [specific safety measures]. Our teams are working to resolve this issue and will continue to provide updates."

3. **Identify and Brief a Spokesperson**
   - Select a credible spokesperson (ideally a high-ranking official) prepared to handle difficult questions with confidence and composure.
   - Equip the spokesperson with key messages, a Q&A document, and talking points to ensure consistent, accurate communication.

4. **Gather Essential Information for Public Communication**
   - Collect accurate details on what happened, the impact on affected parties, and any measures being taken. Use this information to craft responses for media and stakeholders.
   - Prioritize questions about what happened, who is involved, and how the organization is responding.

5. **Utilize Multiple Communication Channels**

- Deploy consistent messaging across all relevant channels, including social media, email, and press releases, to reach varied stakeholders.
- Tailor messages for each audience to ensure that all receive information relevant to their concerns and interests.

6. **Maintain a Calm, Empathetic Tone**

- Strive for a balanced tone that is neither dismissive nor sensational. Emphasize safety, empathy, and actions taken to prevent panic and reassure stakeholders.
- Example: Address concerns by calmly explaining the steps taken to address the crisis and prevent further issues.

7. **Prepare Answers for Business-Related and Stakeholder Questions**

- Anticipate common questions about the crisis impact on employees, customers, operations, and the organization's response.
- Be prepared to address concerns around layoffs, product recalls, operational disruptions, and steps taken to prevent recurrence.

8. **Engage in Proactive Social Listening**

- Monitor social media and traditional media channels to gauge public sentiment and identify emerging concerns or misinformation.
- Adjust messaging as needed to address rumors and keep the public informed.

9. **Update Internal Stakeholders Regularly**

- Keep executives and department heads informed of the crisis response and developments. This ensures alignment and supports unified decision-making.
- Maintain open communication with employees to

keep them reassured and engaged, providing clear instructions and updates as necessary.

10. **Document All Crisis Response Steps for Post-Crisis Review**

   - Track all actions taken, decisions made, and communications released to inform the post-crisis evaluation and identify areas for improvement.
   - Documenting this information provides a foundation for refining the Crisis Communications Plan and improving future responses.

By implementing these takeaways and action items, organizations can effectively manage the initial stages of a crisis, maintain stakeholder trust, and set the stage for a resilient recovery.

PART IV: POST-CRISIS EVALUATION AND LEARNING - THE PATH TO RECOVERY AND CONTINUOUS IMPROVEMENT

After a crisis subsides, it can be tempting to focus solely on returning to normal operations. However, the post-crisis phase is a critical opportunity for reflection, learning, and improvement. Effective post-crisis evaluation not only strengthens future crisis responses but also demonstrates a commitment to transparency and accountability. This chapter outlines a comprehensive approach to post-crisis evaluation, emphasizing the importance of continuous improvement and engagement with stakeholders to restore trust and enhance organizational resilience.

THE RIPPLE EFFECT OF A CRISIS: A CASE STUDY

CityWorks Inc., a prominent utility provider, faced a major crisis when a routine inspection revealed elevated lead levels in the water supply of one of its largest districts. The situation escalated when a resident's social media post about murky tap water went viral, attracting both public and media scrutiny. The crisis damaged CityWorks' reputation, as misinformation and public outrage spread quickly online.

After three weeks of crisis management, CityWorks had contained the immediate threat, but the aftermath presented an opportunity for growth and recovery. Through follow-up communication, stakeholder engagement, and a rigorous post-crisis analysis, CityWorks aimed to turn this challenging experience into a foundation for future resilience.

I. THE IMPORTANCE OF FOLLOW-UP COMMUNICATION AND DELIVERING ON PROMISES

During a crisis, organizations often make promises to address issues, implement corrective measures, or keep stakeholders informed.

Delivering on these promises is essential for rebuilding trust and maintaining credibility. Stakeholders need assurance that their concerns have been taken seriously and that the organization is committed to preventing similar issues in the future.

Key Actions for Follow-Up Communication:

- **Deliver All Promised Information**: Provide any follow-up details promised during the crisis, such as updates on safety measures, corrective actions, or ongoing investigations.
- **Provide Transparency in Recovery Efforts**: Explain what steps are being taken to prevent recurrence, including any ongoing challenges or limitations.

- **Maintain Communication Channels**: Don't assume silence equates to satisfaction. Open lines of communication give stakeholders a chance to ask questions or express remaining concerns.

Maintaining communication, even after the crisis is no longer front-page news, reinforces accountability and reassures stakeholders that the organization values their trust.

II. Keeping Stakeholders Updated on Recovery Progress

A crisis may be officially over, but recovery often involves long-term efforts that stakeholders care about. Regular updates on recovery progress show that the organization is actively working to fulfill its commitments. This is an opportunity to engage stakeholders and demonstrate resilience.

Strategies for Stakeholder Engagement:
- **Periodic Updates**: Provide progress reports on recovery efforts through multiple channels, such as email updates, social media, or the company website.
- **Highlight Positive Developments**: Share milestones and successes within the recovery process to demonstrate progress and inspire confidence in the organization's resilience.
- **Address Remaining Concerns**: Monitor public sentiment and respond to any lingering questions or misconceptions.

Continuous communication during the recovery phase shows stakeholders that the organization is committed to addressing the impacts of the crisis, reinforcing trust and credibility.

III. Conducting a Post-Crisis Evaluation: Lessons Learned and

Process Improvement

Once the immediate crisis has passed, a thorough post-crisis evaluation is essential. This review assesses what went well, identifies areas for improvement, and allows the organization to refine its crisis response strategies.

Steps for Conducting a Post-Crisis Evaluation:

1. **Debrief with Crisis Management and Communications Teams**: Gather all departments involved in the crisis response, including communications, legal, HR, and operations, for an open and honest debrief. Discuss what worked, what didn't, and any obstacles encountered.

2. **Assess Communication Effectiveness**:
   - **Review Internal and External Communications**: Evaluate the timing, accuracy, and clarity of messages for each audience.
   - **Identify Gaps in Messaging**: Look for any communication gaps that may have contributed to confusion or frustration.
   - **Examine Social Media and Public Sentiment**: Evaluate the impact of social media monitoring and engagement. Consider how public sentiment influenced the crisis response and identify areas for improvement in future social media strategies.

3. **Analyze Operational and Logistical Responses**:
   - **Evaluate Speed and Efficiency**: Assess how quickly resources were deployed, protocols implemented, and partnerships coordinated.
   - **Identify Bottlenecks**: Determine where resources may have been insufficient or where internal processes hindered an efficient response.

4. **Gather Stakeholder Insights**:
   - Solicit feedback from customers, employees, and

    partners to understand their perspectives on the organization's crisis response.

- This feedback provides valuable insights into stakeholder needs and helps identify areas for improvement.

5. **Document Lessons Learned**: Summarize key takeaways and identify both strengths and weaknesses in the response. Share insights with leadership and relevant teams to build organizational knowledge.

6. **Update the Crisis Communications Plan**:

- Based on the evaluation, incorporate lessons learned into the Crisis Communications Playbook.
- Update protocols, improve communication strategies, and identify new resources or technologies that could strengthen future responses.

By thoroughly analyzing the crisis and identifying areas for improvement, organizations can transform a challenging experience into a valuable learning opportunity, enhancing resilience for future challenges.

IV. Integrating Lessons into Continuous Improvement

Crisis management is an evolving process. Each incident provides unique insights that contribute to a stronger, more prepared organization.

The goal of the post-crisis phase is not just to return to normal operations but to emerge stronger and better equipped for future challenges.

Key Actions for Continuous Improvement:

- **Regularly Test and Update Crisis Plans**: Schedule regular simulations and training exercises to test the updated Crisis Communications Playbook. Practice is essential for ensuring that new protocols are familiar to the team and that responses are well-coordinated.

- **Monitor Industry Best Practices**: Crisis management techniques evolve rapidly. Stay informed of best practices and technological advances in crisis communications. Consider how new tools or methods could enhance the organization's response capabilities.

- **Foster a Culture of Preparedness**: Encourage employees at all levels to engage in crisis preparedness. A culture that prioritizes awareness and proactive risk management helps organizations stay agile and responsive.

By committing to continuous improvement, organizations can build a foundation for long-term resilience, ensuring they are better prepared to handle future crises.

BUILDING A CULTURE OF CONTINUOUS IMPROVEMENT

The post-crisis phase is a unique opportunity to reinforce an organization's commitment to continuous improvement. When an organization learns from each crisis, refining its practices and building a stronger response framework, it becomes better prepared for future challenges.

By establishing a culture of proactive risk management and readiness, organizations can turn crises into valuable learning experiences that drive long-term resilience.

EMERGING STRONGER FROM EACH CRISIS

The post-crisis phase is far from a mere afterthought. It is a crucial period for reconnecting with stakeholders, evaluating response effectiveness, and refining the crisis management strategy.

By following through on promises, maintaining transparent communication, and committing to continuous improvement, organizations can not only recover but also emerge with a renewed sense of purpose, resilience, and stakeholder trust.

Effective post-crisis evaluation allows organizations to:

- Strengthen crisis management capabilities,
- Enhance future responses,
- Demonstrate accountability and transparency,
- Build lasting trust with stakeholders.

A well-executed post-crisis phase not only repairs the damage from the crisis but also sets the foundation for a more resilient organization. Embracing this process ensures that each crisis becomes a steppingstone toward a more robust, trusted, and adaptable future.

POST-CRISIS FOLLOW-UP CHECKLIST

The following checklist provides a streamlined summary of actions to take during the post-crisis phase:

1. **Deliver on Promises and Maintain Communication**:
   - Fulfill commitments made to stakeholders, such as safety updates or refunds.
   - Keep stakeholders informed about recovery efforts and developments.

2. **Conduct a Comprehensive Post-Crisis Evaluation**:
   - Debrief with all teams involved to assess strengths and areas for improvement.
   - Gather feedback from stakeholders, employees, and customers on the crisis response.

3. **Update the Crisis Communications Plan**:
   - Incorporate lessons learned into the crisis plan.
   - Adjust protocols, refine key messages, and improve training exercises.

4. **Document the Crisis for Future Reference**:
   - Record the timeline, decisions made, and outcomes for internal records.
   - Store communication templates and key documents for future crises.

5. **Monitor Long-Term Effects and Public Sentiment**:

- Track public sentiment and media mentions in the weeks following the crisis.
- Address any lingering concerns or reputation issues through ongoing engagement.

6. **Prepare for Continuous Improvement**:
   - Schedule regular crisis response drills to keep the team prepared and resilient.
   - Stay informed of industry best practices and emerging trends in crisis communication.

Key Takeaways:

1. **Post-Crisis Evaluation is Essential for Growth**: The post-crisis phase offers a crucial opportunity for reflection, learning, and improvement. A well-conducted evaluation strengthens future crisis responses, reinforces organizational resilience, and demonstrates accountability to stakeholders.

2. **Follow-Up Communication Builds Trust**: After a crisis, follow-up communication reassures stakeholders that the organization is fulfilling its commitments and prioritizing transparency. Keeping communication channels open is key to maintaining trust and addressing any residual concerns.

3. **Stakeholder Engagement Supports Recovery**: Regular updates on recovery efforts show stakeholders that the organization is actively working to address the impact of the crisis. Engaging stakeholders in this process can foster a sense of partnership and trust.

4. **Comprehensive Post-Crisis Evaluation Identifies Lessons Learned**: A thorough post-crisis review allows organizations to analyze what went well and where improvements are needed. This process includes reviewing communications, operations, stakeholder feedback, and documenting takeaways for future reference.

5. **Continuous Improvement Reinforces Preparedness**: Incorporating lessons learned into updated crisis plans, conducting regular drills, and staying informed of industry best practices help build a culture of readiness. Continuous improvement ensures the organization emerges stronger and better prepared for future challenges.

6. **Building a Culture of Proactive Crisis Management**: Emphasizing preparedness and risk management across the organization fosters an environment where employees are engaged in preventing and managing crises. A proactive culture helps the organization respond more swiftly and effectively in the face of adversity.

Action Items:

1. **Deliver on Promises and Communicate Regularly**
   - Fulfill commitments made to stakeholders during the crisis, such as updates on safety measures or corrective actions.
   - Keep stakeholders informed about recovery efforts through regular updates across multiple channels (e.g., email, social media).
   - Maintain open lines of communication to address any lingering concerns and ensure stakeholders feel valued.

2. **Engage Stakeholders During Recovery**
   - Provide periodic updates on recovery milestones and achievements to reinforce confidence in the organization's resilience.
   - Address public sentiment and respond to any lingering questions or misinformation to maintain transparency.

3. **Conduct a Comprehensive Post-Crisis Evaluation**
   - Debrief with all teams involved (communications, legal, HR, operations) to assess the effectiveness of the crisis response.
   - Review both internal and external communications, identifying any gaps or areas where messaging could have been improved.
   - Solicit feedback from stakeholders, customers, and employees to gain a comprehensive view of the crisis response.

4. **Update the Crisis Communications Plan**
   - Incorporate insights and lessons learned into the Crisis Communications Playbook, refining protocols and messaging strategies.

- Adjust training exercises and simulations to address any identified weaknesses and ensure the team is prepared for future crises.

5. **Document the Crisis for Future Reference**
   - Record key details such as the crisis timeline, decisions made, and outcomes to create a reference for future crises.
   - Archive communication templates, key documents, and feedback from stakeholders to inform future responses.

6. **Monitor Long-Term Effects and Public Sentiment**
   - Track media coverage and public sentiment for any lasting effects of the crisis, addressing concerns as they arise.
   - Continue engaging with stakeholders if additional issues or questions surface, using these interactions to rebuild trust.

7. **Commit to Continuous Improvement**
   - Schedule regular crisis response drills and simulations to test the updated crisis plan and reinforce team readiness.
   - Stay informed on industry trends and best practices in crisis communication to enhance response capabilities.
   - Foster a culture of preparedness by encouraging employees at all levels to participate in crisis readiness initiatives.

8. **Build a Culture of Continuous Improvement and Crisis Preparedness**
   - Reinforce the organization's commitment to proactive risk management by engaging employees in regular crisis training.
   - Emphasize the importance of learning from each crisis to build resilience and prepare for future challenges.
   - Use each crisis as an opportunity to improve processes

and strengthen the organization's foundation for long-term success.

By focusing on these takeaways and implementing the action items, organizations can turn the challenges of a crisis into valuable learning experiences. This approach not only aids in recovery but also builds a more resilient, trusted, and adaptable organization prepared to face future challenges effectively.

THE IMPERATIVE OF PREPAREDNESS AND EXPERTISE IN CRISIS COMMUNICATION

Crises are increasingly unpredictable and public scrutiny is relentless. The importance of effective crisis communication cannot be overstated. From safeguarding an organization's reputation to protecting financial stability, the way a crisis is communicated can be the difference between a swift recovery and a prolonged reputational, operational, or financial setback.

Organizations today face unprecedented pressures to act quickly, transparently, and responsibly when a crisis occurs. A 2022 survey by PR Week reported that 63% of PR firms have increased their crisis communications staff due to growing client demand, reflecting the rising acknowledgment that crises are inevitable—and that being prepared to handle them is essential. Additionally, data from the U.S. Bureau of Labor Statistics shows that demand for public relations specialists, including crisis communication experts, is expected to grow by 11% from 2020 to 2030, outpacing the average growth for all occupations. This trend underscores the need for seasoned professionals who bring not only technical expertise but also a steady hand in the face of turmoil.

Beyond the walls of the organization, public expectations have also shifted. Edelman's Trust Barometer found that 83% of employees expect CEOs to take action during a crisis—not only to safeguard the business but to address broader societal issues as well.

This expanded expectation places new demands on leaders to navigate crises with sensitivity, transparency, and accountability. In today's social climate, crises often reach beyond the company itself, with consumers, employees, and communities demanding honesty and empathy in times of hardship. The data is clear: 64% of consumers believe brands should communicate openly and honestly during a crisis, according to a study by Sprout Social, and 55% say they would boycott a brand that fails to meet this standard.

However, successful crisis communication doesn't just happen in the heat of the moment; it's built on a foundation of preparation, a clear communication strategy, and the involvement of a capable crisis management team. This playbook has outlined the essential elements of crisis communication—from pre-crisis planning and team building to real-time response and post-crisis analysis— equipping your organization with the tools to respond swiftly and strategically when a crisis arises.

But a playbook is only as effective as the people executing it. The guidance and insights of a seasoned communications professional are invaluable when stakes are high and decisions must be made under pressure. These experts bring more than knowledge; they bring perspective, having navigated similar challenges before. An experienced crisis communicator can anticipate the public's concerns, handle media inquiries with precision, and craft messages that protect the organization's reputation while addressing stakeholder needs.

As crises continue to rise in frequency and complexity, organizations that invest in crisis communication expertise and maintain a well-prepared playbook will not only survive but potentially emerge stronger. A commitment to transparency, empathy, and timely communication can turn even the most challenging situations into opportunities to strengthen trust and loyalty among consumers, employees, and the public.

Crisis communication is not merely a business function; it's a critical component of organizational resilience and reputation management. As you move forward, let this playbook serve as a constant reminder: the cost of silence is far greater than the cost of preparation, and the power of a well-placed word is often the key to navigating the storm.